Autobiographies You Never
Thought You'd Read

THE TOOTH FAIRY

Catherine Chambers

heinemann
raintree

© 2016 Heinemann-Raintree
an imprint of Capstone Global Library, LLC
Chicago, Illinois

To contact Capstone Global Library please call 800-747-4992, or visit our web site www.capstonepub.com

Edited by Linda Staniford
Designed by Steve Mead
Original illustrations © Capstone Global Library Ltd 2015
Illustrated by Christian Suarez - Advocate Art
Production by Victoria Fitzgerald
Originated by Capstone Global Library
Printed and bound in China by Leo Paper Products

19 18 17 16 15
10 9 8 7 6 5 4 3 2 1

Library of Congress Cataloging-in-Publication Data
Chambers, Catherine, 1954-
  The tooth fairy / Catherine Chambers.
     pages cm.—(Autobiographies you never thought you'd read)
  Includes bibliographical references and index.
  ISBN 978-1-4109-7964-3 (hb)—ISBN 978-1-4109-7969-8 (pb)—ISBN 978-1-4109-7979-7 (ebook) 1. Teeth—Juvenile literature. 2. Tooth loss—Juvenile literature. 3. Fairies—Juvenile literature. I. Title.
  GR489.3.C43 2016
  398.21—dc23   2015000254

Acknowledgments
Every effort has been made to contact copyright holders of material reproduced in this book. Any omissions will be rectified in subsequent printings if notice is given to the publisher.

All the Internet addresses (URLs) given in this book were valid at the time of going to press. However, due to the dynamic nature of the Internet, some addresses may have changed, or sites may have changed or ceased to exist since publication. While the author and publisher regret any inconvenience this may cause readers, no responsibility for any such changes can be accepted by either the author or the publisher.

Contents

Some words are shown in bold, **like this**. You can find out what they mean by looking in the glossary.

What Do I Do?

I am the Tooth Fairy. I'm the one who takes your tooth after it falls out. Then I leave a treat in its place. It could be a coin or a small gift. It depends on where I am in the world.

DID YOU KNOW?

Many children sing rhymes to make the Tooth Fairy visit.

What Do I Look Like?

You might have seen me in books or paintings or have read about me in poems and folk tales. All over the world, there are different ideas about me.

In the United States, I have shimmering wings. But in France, I'm a furry mouse!

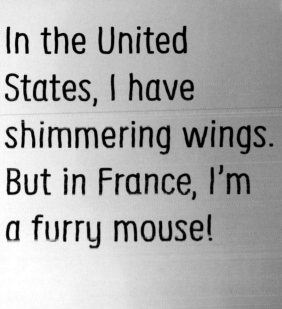

Where Do I Come From?

I think I'll keep that a mystery! But I do travel a lot. I fly from the Americas to Europe. I turn up in Africa and Asia, too.

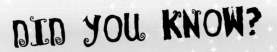

DID YOU KNOW?

I have to know many languages. In French, I'm called "*la petite souris*." This means "the little mouse"!

How Old Am I?

I find it hard to remember how old I am. I know that it was the **Vikings** who brought over the idea of giving money for a tooth to the British Isles, about 1,200 years ago. I know this because I was already around then!

DID YOU KNOW?

Long ago in England, some parents burned their child's tooth. This stopped bad spirits from finding it and casting spells on the child.

Is My Work Hard?

I have to travel a long, long way to find a tooth. Sometimes it's on a roof or even dug into the ground! So, you see, my life isn't easy!

DID YOU KNOW?

Most of you have 20 baby teeth. This means I get to visil you 20 times!

Where Do I Start?

Let me give you an idea of what my work is like. Last night, I was called to **Brazil**. I found a tooth on a hot tiled roof. It shone in the moonlight.

I took the tooth and left a shiny coin.

Then I flew across a huge ocean to **Uganda**. Here, I changed into...

...a rat! I twitched my whiskers and scurried to the corner of a dark room. There, I found a sparkling tooth. I gave some shiny **shillings** for that one!

DID YOU KNOW?

In parts of Africa, it is said that a new tooth won't grow if a lizard sees the old one!

Is It Up High or Down Low?

Next, I jetted off to **Japan**. I searched the roof but found nothing. So I squeezed my wings under the house. Hooray, I found a tooth!

DID YOU KNOW?

In Japan, a lower tooth is thrown on the roof to help the new tooth grow upward. An upper tooth is left under the house, to help the new one grow downward.

Do I Get Thirsty?

I was soon speeding off to snowy **Sweden**. Here, I changed into a mouse. I found a tooth glowing in a glass of water.

I dipped my mouse whiskers into the water and had a long drink. Thank you!

DID YOU KNOW?

I don't always leave a gift behind. In some places, I listen to children's wishes instead.

21

Do I Get Tired?

My last stop was **Sri Lanka**. Phew!
I flew fast across a moonlit sea.

DID YOU KNOW?

Some places have more than one Tooth Fairy creature. In **Greece**, it can be a mouse or a pig!

There I changed into a squirrel and scampered onto the roof. A tooth glowed in the starlight. What a night!

What Do I Do with the Teeth?

In **Turkey**, I might bury a tooth in the yard. But what if the child wants to become a soccer player? Then I bury the tooth in a soccer field, of course!

In parts of South and Central America, I leave the teeth out for mothers to find. They make the teeth into beautiful lucky **charms** for their children.

Do I Take Bad Teeth?

I take all kinds of teeth, but clean, shiny ones are much easier to find. This is why you should always brush your teeth and keep them clean! I know that many of you clean your teeth with a toothbrush.

DID YOU KNOW?

Candy, cookies, and sugary drinks can be bad for us because they make holes in our teeth.

In parts of Africa and the Middle East, children clean their teeth with a special **chewing stick** plucked from a tree.

Do I Really Exist?

What a question! Some people say it is a grown-up who takes the tooth from under the pillow, plucks it from the roof, or digs it up.

DID YOU KNOW?

You might not lose your last baby tooth until you are at least 12 to 13 years old!

28

They think the grown-up then leaves a secret treat behind. Well, that's what I call a fairy tale!

Glossary

Brazil country in South America

charm small piece of jewelry that is worn to protect a person from bad things

chewing stick twig from a special tree in parts of Africa and the Middle East, with juices inside that help to clean teeth

Greece country in southern Europe

Japan country in East Asia

shilling money used in some African countries

Sri Lanka island country south of India

Sweden country in northern Europe

Turkey country in southern Europe

Uganda country in East Africa

Viking invading forces from Norway, in northern Europe, about 1,200 years ago

Find Out More

You could find out more about the Tooth Fairy in other books and on the Internet.

Books

Beeler, Selby B. *Throw Your Tooth on the Roof: Tooth Traditions from Around the World*. Boston: Houghton Mifflin, 2001.

This book will tell you about other tooth traditions.

Diakite, Penda. *I Lost My Tooth in Africa*. New York: Scholastic, 2006.

Find out what happens to Amina's tooth when she goes to Mali, a country in Africa.

Rowan, Kate. *I Know Why I Brush My Teeth*. Cambridge, Mass.: Candlewick, 2000.

Explore the types of teeth and how to take care of them.

Schuh, Mari C. *All About Teeth* (Healthy Teeth). N. Mankato, Minn.: Capstone, 2008.

Learn more about your teeth in this book.

Web sites

Facthound offers a safe, fun way to find Internet sites related to this book. All of the sites on Facthound have been researched by our staff.

Here's all you do:
Visit *www.facthound.com*
Type in this code: 9781410979643

Index